I0462367

Boost Your
Workplace Morale:
A Practical Guide for
Employees
(and their Managers)

BETH BEUTLER

Copyright © 2014 Beth Beutler

All rights reserved.

ISBN: 9781500343729
ISBN 10: 1500343722

Small portions of this book may be shared for the purposes of encouraging others (i.e. within blog posts/social media) but please do not use complete lists or more than a very small portion of the content.)

DEDICATION

To Keith: I'm glad we are on the same team.

CONTENTS

ACKNOWLEDGMENTS

Brenda Covert for editing/proofreading, teaming up with me for a
variety of projects through the years;

My former coworkers in a variety of workplaces that made it fun to be
part of the team;

The employers that allowed me the opportunity to use and strengthen
my teaching and teambuilding skills.

INTRODUCTION

"We're about to implode here. We are overworked, understaffed, underpaid, and not respected or appreciated." That's what someone recently shared with me about his workplace. When I took a poll of my Facebook friends, providing four different topics to help me select what I should develop for my next book, the concept of boosting workplace morale was near the top of the choices. Why?

Morale is a big issue for workplaces today, in part because a less-than-booming economy puts strain on businesses and organizations of all sizes. That leads to heavier workloads, more demands, and less money for raises and extras. Some employees are tired, overworked, underpaid, bored, or unmotivated.

Some may think that the only way to boost morale is to pay an employee more money. Sure, that helps, but even well-paid individuals can be disheartened and discouraged going to their job every day.

Morale goes beyond a paycheck. It reflects a sense of purpose, camaraderie, and value for the lives of employees and the people they serve. It takes effort to build morale, but it doesn't have to take a lot of money. And you don't have to be the owner or a supervisor to influence morale. That's why this book is for anyone who works.

If you work—part time or full time—as an owner, employee, subcontractor, or even a volunteer, you have a say in the morale and culture of that organization. YOU can add some vitality to your workplace culture, no matter how weak or strong you feel it may currently be. That's where this book can help.

The book is divided into thirteen chapters (a baker's dozen, to give you a little more than expected, which is a great way to boost morale as well.) I provide lists of twelve thoughts or ideas related to a particular concept. I've used lists of twelve throughout the book to give you an easy way to incorporate one idea, discussion, or question each month for a year. Many of these ideas can be worked into monthly staff meetings, for example. In addition, at the end of each chapter is a "STAR Step" that anyone can take to "Be a STAR" (Someone That Assists & Refreshes) in the workplace. Take the ideas and modify them to fit your unique situation. Use them to prompt new ideas, discussions, and activities. Do your part (even a small one) to positively enhance your workplace culture.

If you decide you want to go deeper, please visit my website for more details on teambuilding activities and resources. I offer a variety of services that can help you build your team and become more productive. Visit *www.BethBeutler.com* for details.

CHAPTER 1 - 12 WAYS TO BUILD MORALE

1. Pay attention.

Always be on the lookout for appropriate ways to encourage your coworkers. As you pay attention, you'll pick up on their favorite ways to be uplifted (some, for example, may prefer a short note, while others like public recognition) or something that may be troubling them that you can help with.

2. Let joy start with you.

Start your own day with a thankful spirit and let your countenance have a cheerful look. Smile!

3. Ask questions.

When people come to share frustrations, ask questions to guide them in finding a solution, such as "How would it be if you stored the filing cabinet over here instead?" Also ask open-ended questions to show people you are truly interested in them. Instead of, "How was your weekend?" try, "What was the best part of your weekend?"

4. Prepare a "Staff Appreciation Basket."

Fill an attractive basket, tub, or container with a variety of gifts, all costing no more than one to three dollars each. Make sure the gifts are usable or attractive, not tacky. Import stores, home décor stores, craft supply stores, and some dollar stores are good sources of inexpensive but fun gifts. Some gift ideas are small coffee or tea packets, lotions, bath salts, small cans of spray oil, super glue, small tools, upbeat office supplies like bright note pads or interesting writing utensils, gourmet sample foods like crackers, jellies, special candies, candles, etc. Put the container in the break room with a sign that says, "You are appreciated. Grab a gift to enjoy!"

A "Grateful Gift Grab" bucket containing appreciation gifts.

5. Host a contest.

Post a brainteaser on the bulletin board and/or send it around via e-mail once a week. Collect answers. Keep track of points, and give a prize at the end of a certain time.

6. Come up with fun "culture terms" for your office.

For example, in a church office where I used to work, we used acronyms to refer to certain meetings, like "PMS" for Pastoral Ministry Staff or "MASS" for Ministry and Support Staff. Shared language and "inside laughs" are good for bonding.

7. Plan a surprise outing for your coworkers.

Years ago, the work team I was on at the time went to Stone Mountain Park in Georgia. We provided colored   t-shirts for different teams and used the "stone" or "rock" theme as much as possible by providing rock candy, smooth stones with crosses on them (I worked for a church), etc. We played games on the bus and also gave everyone some free time to enjoy the park.

In some cases, you may have to make such outings mandatory and keep them within business hours. Some folks don't enjoy outings or surprises but can often be won over by the end of the day if you are patient with them.

8. Share creative and inspirational stories—cautiously.

Select appropriate, short and verified anecdotes and positive news that you may hear via the media. Be careful with the items you select to share. Don't be preachy, and keep e-mailed items short. Remove all headers (i.e., previous e-mail addresses the stories were sent to) and definitely do not *require* people to forward the stories to others. But the occasional heartwarming story can be a blessing.

9. Affirm a "staff member of the week."

Give others a chance to sign a card for their coworker. Advertise an accomplishment or provide a list of the characteristics others appreciate about him or her. Put the person's picture on a white board and let staff members write compliments to their coworker throughout the week. Then take a photo of it for the individual before erasing it at the end of the week.

Circulate an appreciation card for coworkers to sign. Include a small gift such as a magnet, tea bag or coffee packet.

10. Sponsor secret pals.

Secret pals can be fun but require some commitment. Don't force this on anyone. Keep the term short (such as only one month or for a quarter. A year is too long.) Have a secret pal reveal party at the end of the term. Have one person act as coordinator and send regular reminders to those participating.

11. Encourage wellness.

In one workplace, we had a period of time where people earned "miles" for various healthy habits such as exercise and eating healthy. You can do this and give out a gift for people who earn a certain number of miles, or have prize drawings where individuals earn tickets for particiular milestones. We also had a several-week initiative where staff members signed up to bring in "Tuesday Treats." However, the snacks had to be healthy. Everyone who participated received an entry into a drawing, and the winner received a gift card to a local healthy restaurant.

12. Have an appreciation exchange.

Provide everyone with postcards and draw names. Ask them to write something encouraging to the person whose name they drew before they leave the meeting and then deliver it to that coworker's desk, workspace, or mailbox right after the meeting.

A pat on the back can go a long way.

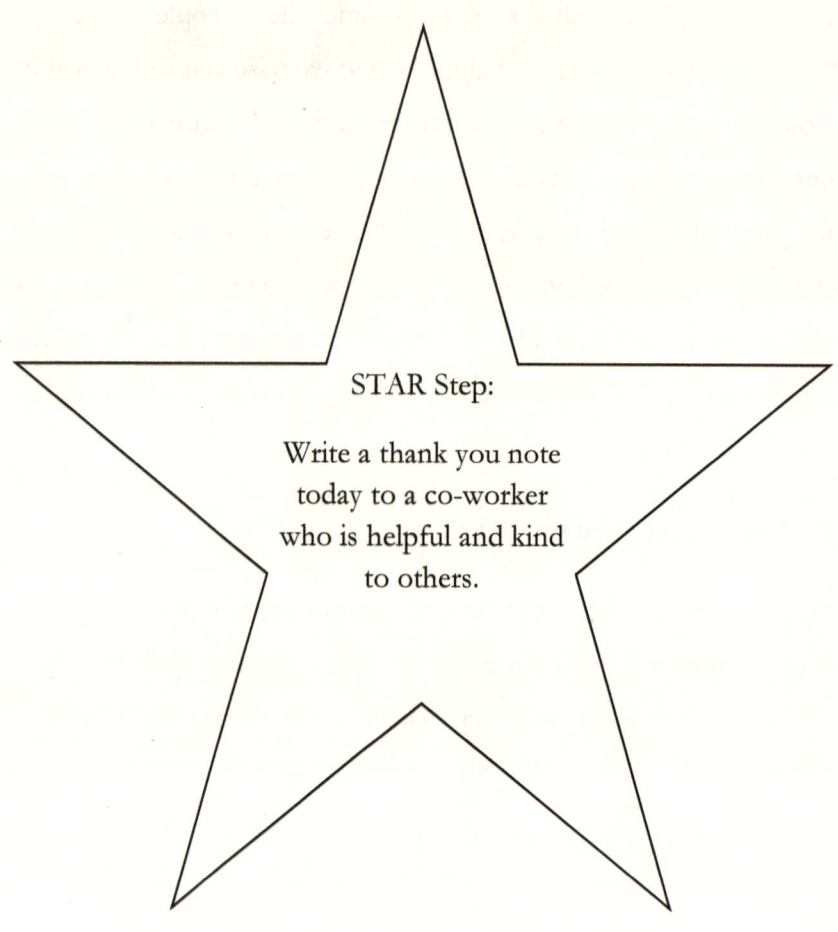

STAR Step:

Write a thank you note
today to a co-worker
who is helpful and kind
to others.

CHAPTER 2 – 12 MORALE OFFICERS

You set the tone. Your attitudes and daily actions play a very important part in building a culture of cooperation, care, and productivity. Which one of these employees are you?

Courteous Cindy

Cindy goes the extra mile to be kind to all coworkers and visitors. She takes a few minutes for a friendly chat with a customer. She picks up items left on the printer and delivers them across the building without complaining. She protects her boss from unnecessary interruptions by graciously screening calls and visitors.

Encouraging Erik

Erik seems to know just the right words to say to someone who is tired, ill, or overwhelmed. He sends encouraging e-mails or stops by to say something uplifting without it coming across as contrived or overdone.

Cooperative Chelsea

Chelsea is willing to lend a hand, regardless of whether the task is on her own to-do list. She helps prepare a mailing. She's willing to cover phones so another coworker can enjoy an uninterrupted hour of work.

She's willing to stay late or come in early on occasion if it will help a big project get done.

Listening Leonard

Leonard has a finely developed listening skill. He hears not just what a person is saying but senses their heart and feelings. He doesn't interrupt to share his responses, and he makes people feel as if they are the only one in the room.

Clean-up Cathy

The break room and common work areas are always presentable because Cathy quietly straightens, wipes, washes, and puts items away whenever she passes through. She is especially attentive to checking these areas before events and times when traffic is expected to be high.

Fun-lover Frank

Frank can always be counted on for infusing a bit of fun into the office. Whether it's a harmless practical joke or a riddle by e-mail, he brings a smile to his coworkers' faces. He knows how to keep from overdoing the joking, treating it more like seasoning than a main course.

Collaborating Callie

Teambuilding is key to Callie. She often leads the staff in fun games, organizes teambuilding exercises, and sends encouraging "atta-boy" or "atta-girl" e-mails. She understands each staff member's personality and knows how to get the staff to work together. She is a great source of fun and laughter and motivates the staff to get things done.

Leader Larry

Larry is a good organizer and motivates people to get involved in worthwhile projects. He seems to be able to jumpstart a team and get them focused into a cohesive unit with one vision.

Warm Wendy

Wendy has the gift of hospitality and sets the tone—or climate—of the office. She brews fresh coffee daily, comes in early to turn on lights, heat, or air-conditioning, and starts background music playing. She waters plants, keeps the bulletin board fresh and informative, and greets everyone with a smile.

Cultivator Charlie

Charlie is great at finding new ways to do things efficiently and enjoys training others. He circulates information about software shortcuts, tips on how to use the copier, and ways to save time. He's able to comb through information and help the staff distill the best tips to improve their efficiency. He's all about helping people grow.

Praise-giving Phyllis

Phyllis is able to notice a person's contribution and positive characteristics and recognize them appropriately for it. Sometimes she will write a short note. Other times she will discreetly point out to the person's supervisor the great job that person did on a certain project. If she thinks it will encourage someone, she will affirm them in person or in public.

Thankful Ted

Ted carries a thankful spirit wherever he goes, and it spills over into the workplace. He rarely complains but instead finds the joy in most situations. Coworkers know not to be negative around Ted. He finds solutions instead of commiserating in whining sessions.

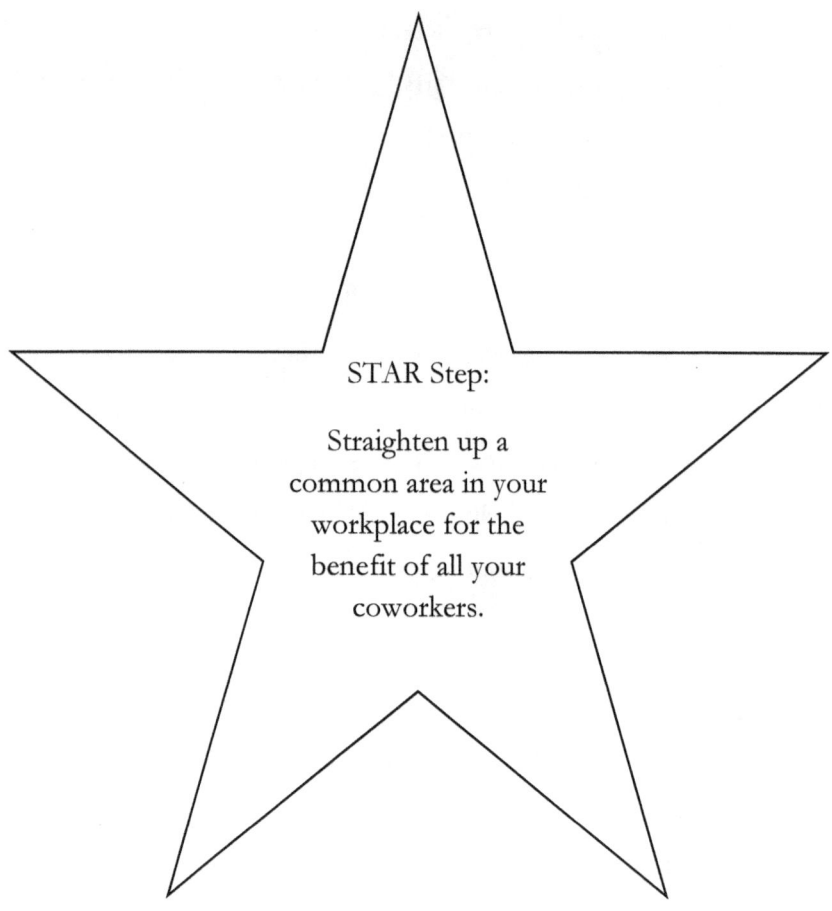

STAR Step:

Straighten up a common area in your workplace for the benefit of all your coworkers.

CHAPTER 3 – 12 WAYS LEADERS RUIN MORALE

I'm talking to you managers, supervisors and team leaders. Here are 12 ways you can ruin morale even if you don't intend to.

1. Don't communicate.

We've all heard of employees who say, "They never tell us anything," or "I never know what's going on." Don't let that be said of you. Instead, set up regular communication opportunities such as smartly-run meetings, weekly summaries, an active Intranet, etc. Don't be afraid to share some of the bad news of running a business. Rumors flow in a vacuum. Better to be upfront (with appropriate respect for confidentiality) with company news—good or bad.

2. Never treat your staff to anything.

Some of the most enjoyable places to work treat their employees to various perks. They don't have to be expensive, but little things make a difference. For example, a monthly breakfast or birthday cake, free coffee, occasional small gifts, or a bit fancier office supplies can all send the message that you care about the environment your employees have to work in.

3. Micromanage and contact your employees at all hours.

I heard about a boss who expected his employee to cc: him on every e-mail the employee sent. Not only does this demonstrate a lack of trust, it gives so much more distraction to the leader who should be focusing on the tasks and projects only he/she can do. I've also heard of a boss who decided that texting his support staff whenever he had an idea was the "hi-tech" way to communicate. The problem? It causes employees to want to avoid answering their phones, it puts the responsibility of managing his ideas onto other people, and it requires them to use a device THEY probably pay for to complete tasks their business requires (without providing them the equipment).

4. Don't empower your employees.

Policies and guidelines are important, but there are times they don't fit a situation. For example, never offering refunds may help you avoid being taken advantage of, but if a front-line employee can't ease the legitimate complaint of a customer, the negative press you may receive is even worse.

5. Never invest in their professional development, especially if they are support staff.

Do you know how demoralizing it can be for support staff to see management go to conferences in lovely places two-three times a year, while the support staff cannot even attend an extended lunch-and-learn opportunity or receive a company-paid-for subscription to a professional development resource? Every employee should have an IDP—an Individual Development Plan that increases their knowledge, certifications, and expertise. I know of one employee of a non-profit organization whose job is database management and integrity. Within her job description is the expectation that she attend a yearly conference sponsored by the software company. This keeps her up to date and also allows her to attend various workshops to enhance her job. It also sends a message that the organization realizes how important her responsibilities are.

6. Never do anything fun and keep the environment sterile.

Yes, your workplace should be productive. But some of the most productive workplaces are those that infuse some fun into the atmosphere. You can offer little contests, motivation for reaching wellness goals, or teambuilding activities at the beginning or end of a staff meeting. You can allow employees some freedom to decorate their cubicle or office, within reason. Professional doesn't have to mean sterile.

7. Overload your employees.

A big morale buster is to overload employees with unreasonable workloads and expectations. There are only so many widgets that can be made in an hour, no matter how many promises your sales people have made. When the workload is too high, quality suffers. People find shortcuts. And that can lead to sloppy work and mistakes that take even more time to fix (not to mention be potentially dangerous if the product is related to health or transportation, for example). Meet regularly with employees to determine how their workflow is going. Shadow them for an hour or more to see how long certain tasks actually take. When people retire or quit, don't just automatically spread the work to remaining staff members to save that salary. Yes, you can make adjustments, and many employees do waste time, but you need to effectively evaluate what is going on and not make hasty decisions without employee input.

8. Ignore personality differences and don't consider best-fits.

Each person brings a unique personality to the workplace. If you choose not to learn about the individual strengths and weaknesses of your team members, you'll tend to make blanket decisions without capitalizing on the strengths and working with the challenges. When a person is made to operate outside of their natural bent continually, morale will deteriorate. Instead, find ways to put people into positions that most match their skills, personalities, and interests.

9. Neglect your own morale.

If you are a leader and *your* morale is poor, your employees will pick up on that. What cheers you up? Do you need to take a walk? Treat yourself to lunch? Set limits on your own workload? Do it! Set an example.

10. Don't set healthy boundaries.

When you expect your employees to work all hours or on weekends to get the work done and don't encourage them to stick with regular business hours, you are empowering them to overdo it and develop a fatigued, angry attitude. I know of a business where employees come in on evenings and weekends, and the leadership allows it. If I were consulting them on this issue, I would suggest they send a message to their employees that late night and weekend work is not looked upon as impressive but rather a sign of too heavy a workload or perhaps a need for some improvement in how they manage their time. I'd even go so far as to make it a rule that work outside the normal hours must be approved first. This can make employees get their work done in the allotted time and/or not provide employees that tend to be martyrs the opportunity to get attention.

11. Never promote or give more responsibility.

Sometimes it is easy to overlook the faithful, behind-the-scenes employees who for months or years have done the same tasks repeatedly. When you are looking to fill positions, remember to start by looking at your current staff and giving them an opportunity to make a change. You could be surprised by someone who is ready to step up to a different level.

12. Talk behind their backs (negatively).

Obviously, you will sometimes have to have personnel discussions and will be talking about your employees from time to time. But always remain professional and discreet, particularly if you have to deal with the negative side of issues. Never put yourself in a position where an employee—or other employees—may overhear you bad-mouthing or gossiping about someone behind their back. You will break trust quickly, which is very hard to rebuild.

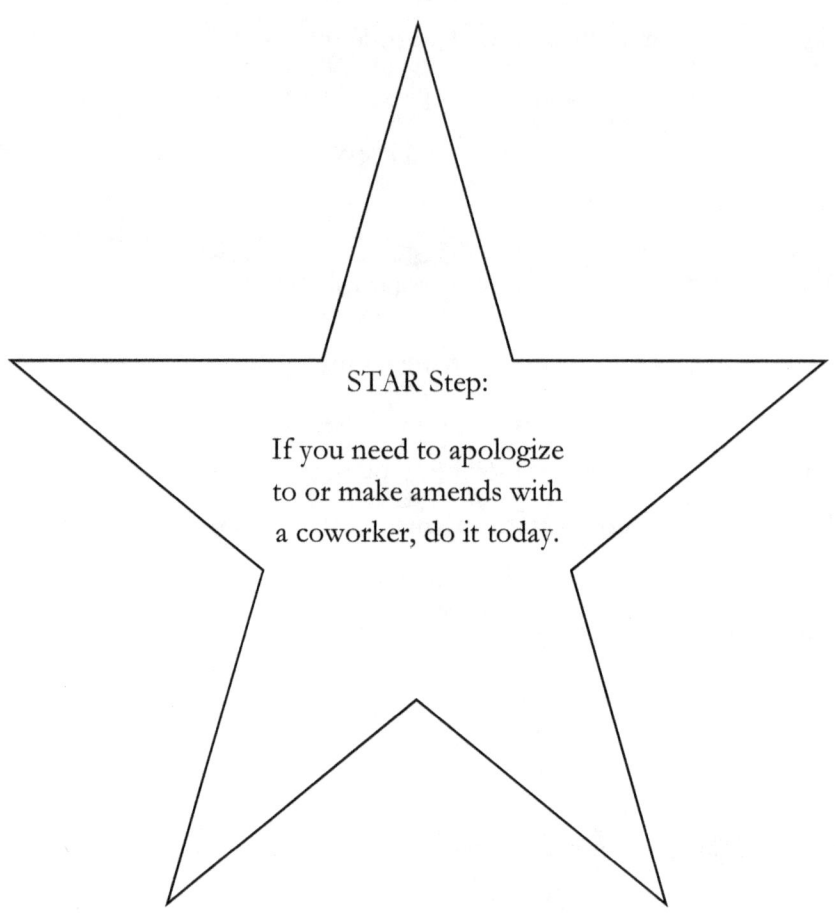

STAR Step:

If you need to apologize
to or make amends with
a coworker, do it today.

CHAPTER 4 – 12 WAYS YOU CAN GET ALONG BETTER WITH YOUR COWORKERS

1. Develop a better understanding of the personality traits of those with whom you work.

Groups who take personality tests and then discuss the results can gain valuable insight into their members. (I offer a simple and fun test at *www.BethBeutler.com*.) There are many things you can learn from such an exercise.

2. Develop a better understanding of yourself.

Give some thought to what irritates you and find ways to reduce those pet peeves. For example, if you get stressed on your commute and arrive grumpy to work each morning, consider adjusting your route or the time you leave. If news radio gets you angry, switch to music, books, or podcasts.

3. Adjust your interactions to match the personality of the person with whom you are speaking.

This doesn't mean you have to completely avoid being yourself. It means, though, that you are willing to temper your extremes if it will result in a more positive relationship. For example:

- If the person favors the "bottom line" with information, don't annoy them with a lot of details, rationale, and feelings, which can eat up a lot of time in conversation

- If the person is detail-oriented, be sure to include at least a few thoughts about why a project needs to be done, along with specific needs and deadlines

- If a person is an introvert, do not force them to get up in front of a group. Instead, draw them out one-on-one

- If a person is an extrovert, give them a chance to lead projects and team meetings rather than make them sit still and listen every time.

4. Remember that any good trait, taken to an extreme, can become annoying. For example:

- friendly and conversational can turn into interfering and domineering

- quiet and observant can turn into aloof and judgmental

- take charge and decisive can turn into impetuous and unfeeling

- detailed and competent can turn into nitpicky and arrogant.

5. Give sincere and specific compliments.

Instead of saying, "Susie, you are so nice!" say, "Susie, I noticed you stop to pick up coffee for everyone even though I know you have a tight schedule. That is very thoughtful. Thank you." Do this on occasion and with sincerity—avoid flattery. Not only will the person feel encouraged, it will often strengthen the relationship between the two of you. Make a list containing at least three good things you like about every coworker. Yes, every one of them. Keep this handy for when it's time to gift someone with a compliment.

6. Practice anonymous acts of kindness.

Don't draw attention to yourself. Do nice things without expectation of favors being returned. It will help you feel good and strengthen positive feelings toward others. You may want to put a reminder on your calendar to do one nice thing per week or month for your coworkers. This doesn't have to be extravagant. Perhaps you could clean up the break room or bring in a treat.

7. Handle conflict quickly and effectively.

Conflict management has been the subject of entire books. These are just a few quick tips:

- Walk away—initially—if you need to cool down.

- After cooling down, resolve issues with people quickly so you— and they—don't stew.

- Don't make the problem bigger than it is. Focus on the specific issue or behavior and don't assume motives or other character traits.

- Avoid generalizing. (e.g., "She is always loud" or "He is never here on time.") Again, deal with the specific behavior or incident.

- Once you've discussed it and reached a resolution—or mutual acceptance that the relationship will never be deep or close—try not to let that influence your future interactions with the person. Believe the best as best you can and treat them with dignity. Not everyone has to be your best friend.

- Confine discussion of the conflict to those directly involved (which may include a trusted individual to act as an objective coach) unless and until you need to go to the next level (i.e., to a supervisor).

8. Don't participate in gossip.

When someone gossips to you, respond by offering to go with them to the person they are talking about, or say something like, "I'm sorry that is your experience with them. Mine has been positive." Keep confidences. If someone is not part of the problem or the solution, consider keeping your thoughts to yourself.

9. Do your part.

If you have agreed to be somewhere by a certain time, be on time or early so you don't make others wait. Fulfill your promises on deadlines. Don't ask others to help you with things you can do yourself, such as asking for information you could easily and quickly search for yourself.

(There's a reason the site *www.lmgtfy.com* was created. Check it out.)

10. Pay attention.

Many of our communication problems come from not listening, reading, or absorbing information well because we are too busy thinking of several other things at the time. Be sure to read memos and instructions carefully. Give your full attention to someone while in a meeting with them. Repeat back what you understand them to mean. This can go a long way toward avoiding conflict and misunderstandings.

Also, pay attention to what people may be going though that may contribute to their behaving in a touchy or unkind manner. While misbehavior and bad attitudes need to be dealt with, there are often underlying circumstances such as illness, financial problems, or family issues that cause people to be distracted and edgy.

11. Be responsive and organized.

Despite all the communication tools we have, it is amazing how many e-mails and messages go into some black hole, never to be seen or responded to. Don't become known as someone who may not return calls or messages. Empty your inbox and voice mail box regularly so no one ever gets a message that it's full and out of room for their message.

Acknowledging an e-mail with a simple "thanks" confirms you've seen it and saves a copy in your "sent" messages. Be able to locate items others need and provide a refreshing environment in your cubicle or office.

12. Don't take the bait.

Some people love to start a quarrel. Be gracious and bite your tongue. Speak up with appropriate assertiveness when you need to, but realize that there are many times that it's just not worth arguing. Most people are entrenched in their opinions (even you), so choose your battles. Sometimes the wisest and strongest "winner" of an argument is the one who doesn't engage in one in the first place.

Sometimes the wisest and strongest "winner" of an argument is the one who doesn't engage in one in the first place.

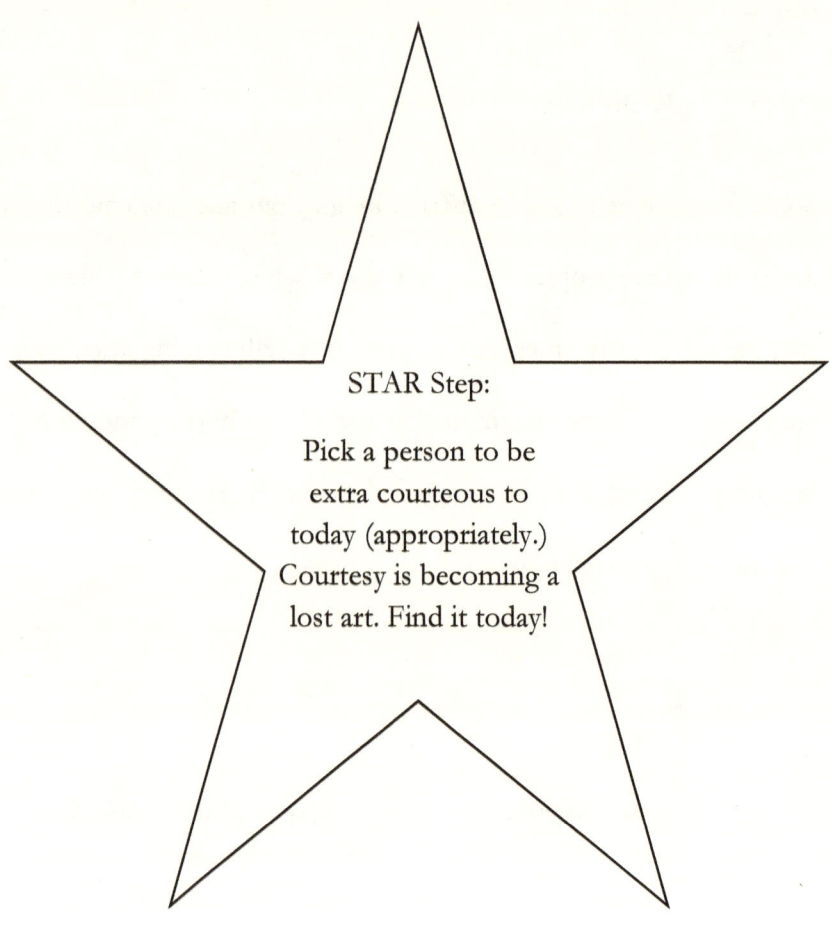

STAR Step:

Pick a person to be
extra courteous to
today (appropriately.)
Courtesy is becoming a
lost art. Find it today!

CHAPTER 5 - 12 ICEBREAKER ACTIVITIES

Icebreaker activities are a great way to build a bond and friendship within your coworkers. Resurrect these as you add new staff members so your group can continue to get to know one another. Pay close attention to the interactions that develop with these icebreakers. They can give insight into the makeup of your staff.

1. Have everyone remove one item from their purse or wallet that represents something important to them. Have each person explain the meaning of the item.

2. Find out one interesting but unknown fact about each person on your staff. Put the facts on index cards and distribute them at the next meeting. (Don't include names.) Ask people to match each fact to the appropriate person.

3. Taking turns, have each staff member turn to the person on their right and ask them to identify their favorite animal, color, number, etc. After the person answers, they must turn to the person on their right and ask a similar question. It cannot be the same question as the one they were asked.

4. Get some old newspapers and magazines. Have each person cut out a picture, headline, or words that represent something about how they feel that day.

5. After everyone is seated for a class or meeting, ask them to get up and move to another location near someone they don't normally sit with, or by someone they don't know as well. Then, have each person use a conversation starter to have a brief "getting to know you" discussion.

6. Ask each staff member to share the name of a historical figure they admire and why.

7. Have each staff member wear a t-shirt to the next staff meeting that represents a team they support, an activity they enjoyed, a vacation they went on, etc.

8. Provide a selection of different colors of card stock. Ask the staff members to select a color that represents them or how they are feeling that day.

9. Ask employees to share where they would go on vacation if they were forced to spend $3,000 and be gone for a week.

10. Ask staff members what they would do for a living if they already had all the money they would ever need.

11. Have a "Fun Facts Scavenger Hunt" where staff members have to find others who fit the categories (e.g., someone wearing red, someone who had spaghetti sometime this week, someone who has more than two pets).

12. Ask employees to share which of their tasks is the most enjoyable, and which is the least.

A sample scavenger hunt list:

- Paperclip chain
- Blue and white coffee mug
- 1966 coin
- Piece of mulch
- Treat from a vending machine
- Digital photo of a particular employee
- Yellow pen
- Key to a shed
- Photo of a particular make/model of car
- Signature of a supervisor

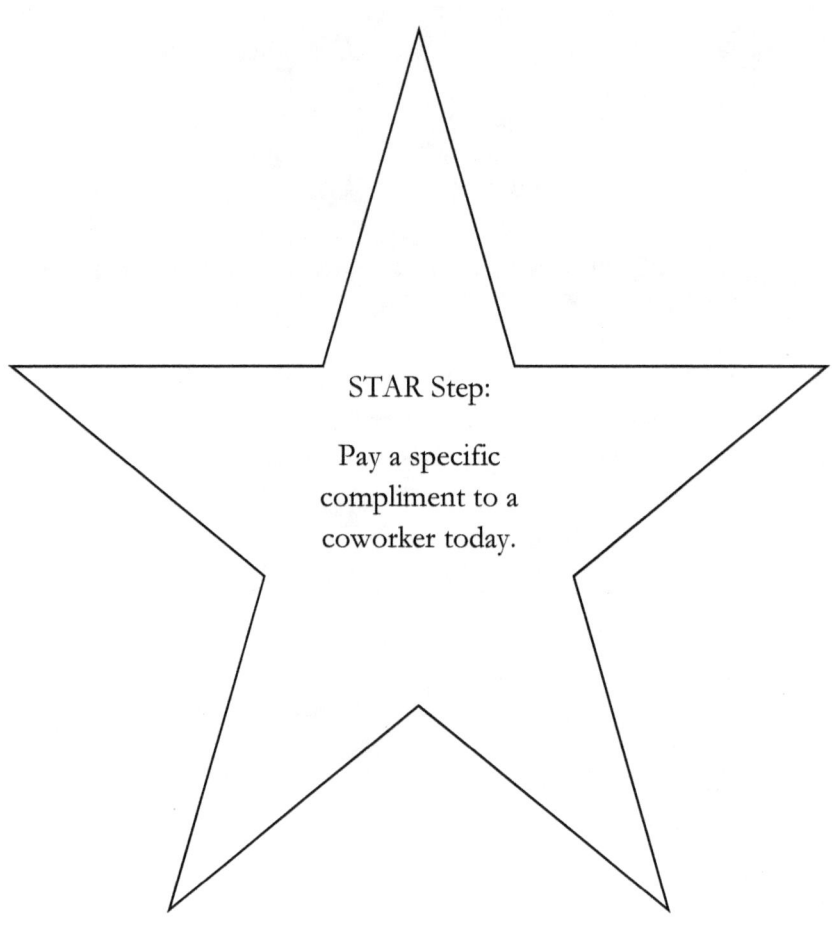

STAR Step:

Pay a specific
compliment to a
coworker today.

CHAPTER 6 – 12 IDEAS FOR TEAMBUILDING GAMES

The following are 12 different initial ideas on which you can build your own teambuilding game. Books and webpages are available with additional instructions, and the next chapter also provides some specific games. This chapter provides the building blocks.

1. Puzzle assembly

Obtain puzzles of various levels of difficulties and create games that challenge people either individually or in groups.

Variations:

- divide staff into teams
- require groups to be silent while assembling
- give teams two minutes to strategize the approach before starting
- have individuals from different teams compete with specific challenges.

Be sure to discuss observations, tying them to communication and leadership concepts.

You can also designate a table in a common area for the ongoing assembly of a challenging puzzle. Allow staff to work on it a few minutes at a time or perhaps as they pass by. Offer a reward at the end of a period of time (e.g., two weeks) if the entire puzzle is assembled. A variation would be to put a few pieces of the puzzle in each staff member's mailbox with the challenge to have the puzzle completed by the end of the month. The reward could be treats like ice cream cones.

2. Balloon games

There are a number of teambuilding activities using balloons. Sometimes the simplicity of blowing up a balloon and quietly tossing it up in "cubicle land" for people to volley about can break up a day's monotony. One warning … if you choose to use teambuilding games that may also involve popping the balloons, be sure to let security know about this. Several popping sounds can cause unnecessary alarm. Also be aware that some folks really have an aversion to having to pop balloons or are easily startled by the noise.

3. Card games

You can use cards to have teams build poker hands or other sequences. These are opportunities for timed teamwork and building strategy and communication skills.

4. Get to Know Me

Using a number of different icebreakers, give your staff the opportunity to get to know one another on a different level than usual. For example, you could have them share a little-known fact about themselves, going around the circle prior to a staff meeting. You can collect questionnaires with lists of topics like favorite vacation spots, hobbies, or movies and try to guess which questionnaire belongs to which staff member.

5. BINGO

Design a bingo card where staff members have to find others who match the topic. These can include things like the person who drives the farthest to work or the individual who had a peanut butter and jelly sandwich for lunch this week.

6. Scavenger Hunt

People always seem to enjoy scavenger hunts, and you can make them simple or elaborate. Think of items that can be easily found in a workplace and that won't require much disruption to retrieve.

7. Communication Relay

Similar to the telephone game, come up with an important but fake announcement and write it on a portable white board. Make sure there are enough words in the announcement to represent the number of staff members playing. Pass the board from one staff member to another, requiring each to change one word in the announcement. Have fun seeing how silly the announcement gets, and then make the point that a small change or misinterpretation of information can eventually make for a major error.

8. Team Identity and Cohesion

Allow departments or small groups to be a team for a certain period of time (e.g., for a three-day workshop), with assignments each day or each week for a month. Assignments can include:

- come up with a team name/logo and make a sign representing it
- decorate your team area to reflect your identity/dress in a certain way to identify the team
- decide on ways to serve the "customers" (which in this case would be other employees)

I used this exercise in a three-day training workshop at a manufacturing plant, and it went over wonderfully. The assigned teams came up with themes that they carried out for the entire workshop. They brought in gifts and snacks to serve others, dressed in similar attire, and came up with fun mottos.

A table decorated by a team using a beach theme.

9. Earn Tickets

Get a roll of raffle tickets and come up with a variety of ways to earn them. My workshop participants went crazy earning tickets for a chance to win a gift card. Tickets can be earned by being on time or early to work or meetings, helping someone else, volunteering to give a summary of a concept, etc. Be generous with the tickets and give away a nice prize at a certain time.

10. Crosswords and Word Finds

Using online puzzle creators, make up word find and crossword puzzles that tie in with your company values, mission statement, team member's names, etc. Allow people to work on these before a staff meeting and then put completed puzzles in a box for a prize drawing.

11. Spend the Money

Divide the staff into groups and give them several hundred dollars of play money. Tell them they are to come up with a budget to spend the money on things of value for the rest of the staff.

12. Make a Logo for Yourself

Encourage staff members to come up with a logo that represents themselves as a company. This may best be done over time. Encourage them to do a quality job and then hang the logo by their nameplate on their cubicle or door.

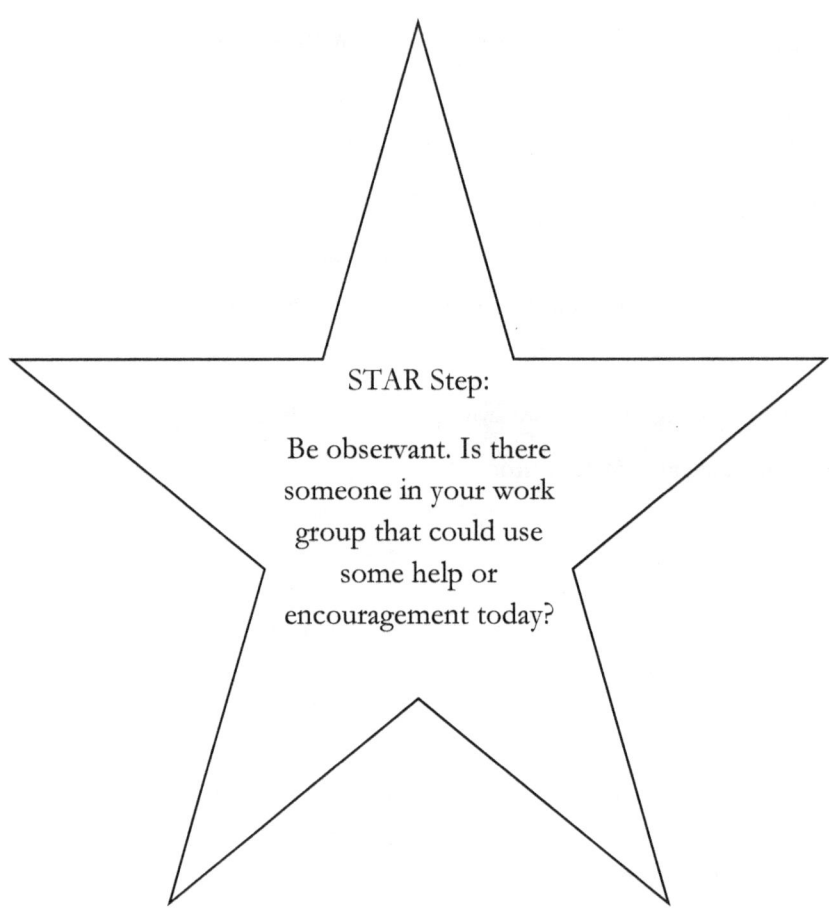

STAR Step:

Be observant. Is there someone in your work group that could use some help or encouragement today?

CHAPTER 7 – 12 SPECIFIC TEAMBUILDING GAMES

The following are specific games you can use with your team. Each includes the objectives for the game and three suggestions or benefits to appreciate as you observe/debrief the activity.

1. Puzzle-in-Progress

Objective: teamwork, showing everyone is needed

Keep a puzzle-in-progress in a break room or common area. Give each staff member a few pieces of the puzzle and challenge the staff to have it finished within a certain time period (e.g., one week, two weeks, one month).

If the puzzle is completed in the allotted time, celebrate with treats. You could also treat the finished puzzle with glue and have it framed for the office.

Debriefing: watch for people working together, attitudes about participating, and those who take charge (e.g., who encourage people to bring their pieces to the table)

2. Affirmation Relay

Objective: recognizing each other's strengths

Give each staff member a card with another staff member's name on it. Have each person write a one-sentence affirmation or one word description of the individual and then pass the card to the next person to do the same thing. The last person to get the card should be the staff member it is addressed to. This is particularly good to do when that staff member is on vacation or out; the card can either be mailed to their home or placed in their company mailbox.

Debriefing/benefits: gives people an opportunity to look for the good in people they work with; opens the minds of others to something they may not have noticed about the person; and allows you to see whether there are issues that make it difficult for people to find anything positive to say about the individual

3. Creative Thinking

Objective: strengthening creativity

Purchase or make magnets with words on them for the break room refrigerator. Encourage staff to form sentences or phrases while waiting for coffee or food to be ready.

Debriefing/benefits: exercises the mind in a different way than their normal job might; provides for some quick team work; can reveal humor

4. Have a Ball!

Objective: get to know people a bit more deeply

Purchase beach balls and write questions on them with a permanent marker. Circle the questions. At a meeting, toss the ball around, asking people to answer the question that ends up closest to their right hand. Questions can include topics such as favorite book, vacation spot, or music; a color to describe themselves; or what they had for breakfast this morning. Search the Internet for balls that can be purchased with prompters already imprinted on them.

Debriefing/benefits: allows staff to get to know each other a little more deeply; draws out people who don't usually share much about themselves; allows people to know better what a person may appreciate for a gift/acknowledgement

5. Treasure Hunt

Objective: learn more about the organization

Investigate the history of your organization and provide small treasures at pertinent spots in your workplace. Provide a sheet with sentences such as "You'll find something sweet at the part of the building that was dedicated in 1947." Alternatively, you could provide a quiz that requires some research or a tour of the building for the questions to be answered.

Debrief/benefits: helps employees understand the history and values behind the workplace; breaks up possible monotony in a day; provides a unique way to offer small affirmations

6. Guess Who?

Objective: gain deeper knowledge of one another

Collect interesting and preferably unknown facts about other staff members. Feature these facts on a bulletin board, white board, or via a weekly e-mail, and reveal the staff member they apply to the following week. Allow staff members to take guesses.

Debrief/benefits: encourages staff to have more than surface conversations; develops appreciation for skills and background that may not otherwise be revealed; helps supervisors know more about their staff and possible areas of strength

7. This is the Way We Build the Company

Objective: teamwork

Purchase some type of toy blocks or building materials. Give small groups an allotted time to assemble a building that most matches the one you work in. Specify that every member of the group must participate.

Debrief/benefits: discuss how each group approached the project; notice details that may have been included; watch who leads and who follows.

8. True or False

Objective: effective communication; proofreading practice

Make a list of upcoming events or instructions that need to be communicated to your workers or customers. Purposefully falsify a few of the facts. Test your staff on whether the information on the piece is correct. Make sure you destroy the false ones before finalizing anything official!

Debrief/benefits: helps staff develop a keener eye for editing/proofreading; demonstrates the importance of clear communication; opens door to discuss problems that could arise from unclear communication

9. I Need You/I Trust You

Objective: teamwork, planning, trust

Plan ahead on this one. Decide on a special snack (e.g., ice cream sundae bar) for the staff but do not announce its availability to everyone. Instead, provide the information to a select few who will be responsible for preparing the snack and then communicating its availability. Give only part of the items or information to each of those chosen individuals (for example, to one, give instructions as to where to find the ice cream, to another, where to find the toppings, and so on). Tell them they must work together to get the snack prepared and keep it secret until it's ready. This will require them to plan and execute the treat without talking about it around others.

Debrief/benefits: teaches the value of confidentiality; requires people to work together, merging their part of the job into the whole; helps leaders to see who steps up to do their assignment and who does not contribute well

10. Trading Spaces

Objective: gaining a new perspective

Warning: this is for brave leaders!

Pick a day when staff members will trade workspaces for a period of time (e.g., two hours). This may put support staff in a boss's office and vice versa! The staff member is to leave a project that the other person can do for them during that time (such as filing or having to make a budgetary decision).

Note: you must make the tasks appropriate and fall within the lines of confidentiality. For example, if someone trades and ends up as HR Director for two hours, rather than working with official files, give them mock duties that would be similar to what the director does daily.

Debriefing/benefits: may prompt a great discussion about what roles each person plays; can show tasks that may be tedious and unappreciated; can reveal how long a task actually takes

11. Service Stand

Objective: learning to serve others and watch for ways to help; brainstorming

Assign a small group of staff members to come up with a way to serve others (coworkers and/or customers) on a particular day of the month. If you have enough staff members, assign one month to each group. If possible, provide a budget (e.g., $100) to the group to use to get supplies. Let the groups be creative, but if you need some ideas to prompt them, they could:

- Set up a coffee, tea, or lemonade stand
- Deliver treats to each workstation
- Arrange to have a mobile car wash come and wash cars while people are working
- Invite a special guest to come perform—e.g., a musician during lunch time or a singer to walk the halls

Debrief/benefits: strengthens brainstorming ability; allows people to work both in front and behind scenes; puts focus on others

12. Conquer Conflict

Objective: conflict management

Research role plays of different conflict situations or come up with scenarios (e.g., an unhappy customer). Have staff members act out ways to resolve the conflict and practice them in front of other coworkers who are allowed to coach. Tell coaches they have to give at least two affirmations and at least one constructive idea or critique regarding how the actors did.

Debrief/benefits: helps people discuss a difficult topic; equips people with possible responses to be prepared before conflict occurs; may address some actual conflict occurring

Games can be a great way to ease stress and get to know other coworkers in a different context.

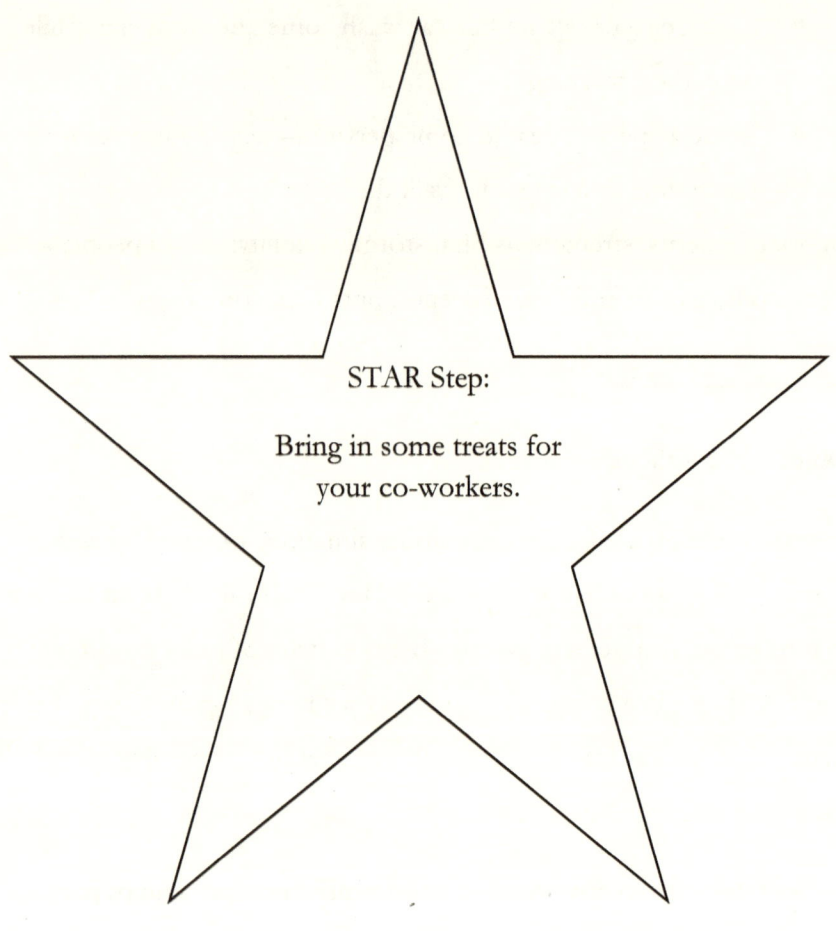

STAR Step:

Bring in some treats for
your co-workers.

CHAPTER 8 – 12 OUTINGS TO ENJOY WITH YOUR COWORKERS

These ideas will be even more effective if the employer is willing to pick up part or all of the cost but don't let that stop you!

1. Have a holiday party at a nice venue.

2. Enjoy a picnic lunch on the grounds or at a local park. You could book a food truck or an ice cream truck to meet you at your location or the park.

3. Take families to an amusement park for the day.

4. Go to a dressy cultural event (e.g., a theatre or musical event).

5. Cheer on a local sports team. (i.e. baseball, football, or hockey).

6. Take part in a sports activity together (e.g., volleyball, bowling).

7. Set up an opportunity for staff to serve in the community and don't dock hours for doing it.

8. Go on a retreat. If appropriate, include spouses.

9. Schedule a quarterly dinner at a variety of restaurants in your area.

10. Visit a local attraction like a museum or historic site or take a tour of a non-profit organization doing good work in your community.

11. Do a "small business" scavenger hunt where employees have to go to local businesses to retrieve items/gifts you have already paid for in advance.

12. Arrange a monthly "Breakfast with the Boss" for a small group of staff members to have breakfast in a conference room with one of the company's management team.

Outings give people an opportunity to show other sides of their personality and build a sense of belonging.

STAR Step:

Volunteer to plan an outing for your coworkers or plan a gathering off hours.

CHAPTER 9 – 12 BUSINESS-FOCUSED CONVERSATION STARTERS FOR STAFF MEETINGS

It's important to have—and keep—open communication with your staff and questions like these can help. To avoid having people feel put "on the spot," provide a way for them to respond anonymously prior to the meeting; you would then read the responses at the meeting. Or, send out a question along with any reminders of an upcoming meeting. This will give people time to ponder their answers and allow the conversation to go deeper than it might if you just pop the question at staff meeting.

1. What does our company do best?

2. Where is our area of greatest need for improvement?

3. What is one task that we could possibly stop doing without serious ramifications?

4. What are some new ways we can serve our clients/customers?

5. What policy is hampering our effectiveness as a team?

6. What idea has allowed you to do something more efficiently and save time/effort?

7. What new piece of equipment would be helpful to add to our company?

8. What is one of your pet peeves in regard to this workplace?

9. What concerns do you have about workload? Are some overloaded while others are bored?

10. What do you appreciate about the person to your right?

11. Which values of our company are we demonstrating most effectively? Which ones are being neglected?

12. Take some time to discuss the results of the personality assessment. (There is one available at *www.BethBeutler.com*.)

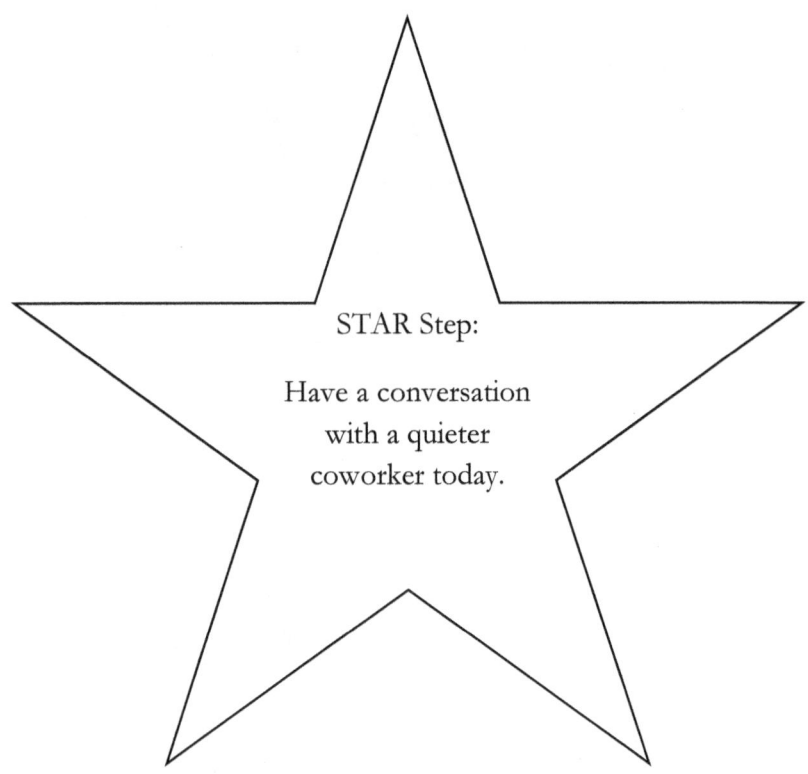

STAR Step:

Have a conversation
with a quieter
coworker today.

CHAPTER 10 – 12 CONVERSATION STARTERS FOR INFORMAL GATHERINGS

These prompters are less serious than the ones designed to promote business discussions. Use these during informal meals or retreats or around the coffee maker!

1. What's been the best part of your day so far?

2. What was the most unique thing you did last week?

3. What would "make your day" today?

4. How have you grown this week?

5. If you were on vacation today, where would you be?

6. If money were not an object, what would you be doing today?

7. What has been your favorite place to live?

8. If you could make one change to your home, what would it be?

9. What has been one of your most significant experiences?

10. If I were to take you to lunch, where would be the first place you'd suggest?

11. What is your favorite holiday, and why?

12. What is one of your fondest memories from childhood?

Questions are such a valuable tool. They help defuse defensiveness, draw out ideas, and display your willingness to consider other people's viewpoints—if you ask them with the right motive and with appropriate respect.

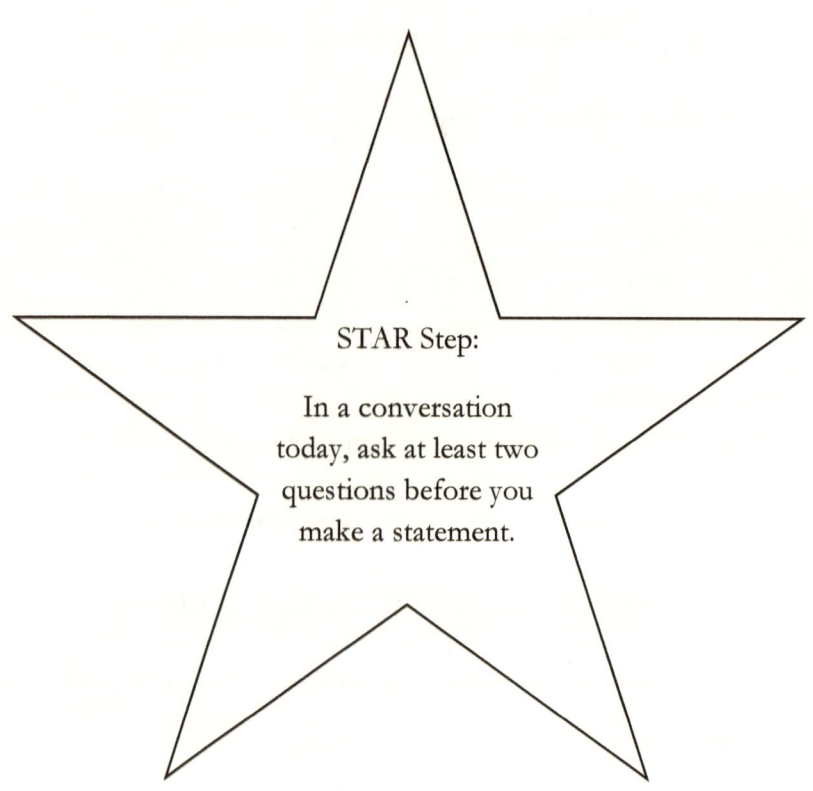

STAR Step:

In a conversation today, ask at least two questions before you make a statement.

CHAPTER 11 – 12 USEFUL ITEMS FOR FUN AT THE WORKPLACE

Keep these items on hand. They can be valuable for creative teambuilding or just plain fun! You might want to keep a bright box or container full of fun things like this to pull out during staff meetings or other gatherings.

1. Pipe cleaners

2. Clay or soft modeling dough

3. Paper clips of various sizes and colors

4. Crayons/markers

5. Different types of paper: construction, patterned, cardstock

6. Stickers, stamp pads, stamps

7. Building blocks/toys

8. Ribbon/yarn

9. Tape, glue, staplers

10. Natural items like twigs and stones

11. Miscellaneous items like feathers, buttons, glitter

12. Scissors of various types

Some people are kinesthetic learners, meaning it is helpful for them to learn by doing. Tangible objects can help facilitate that.

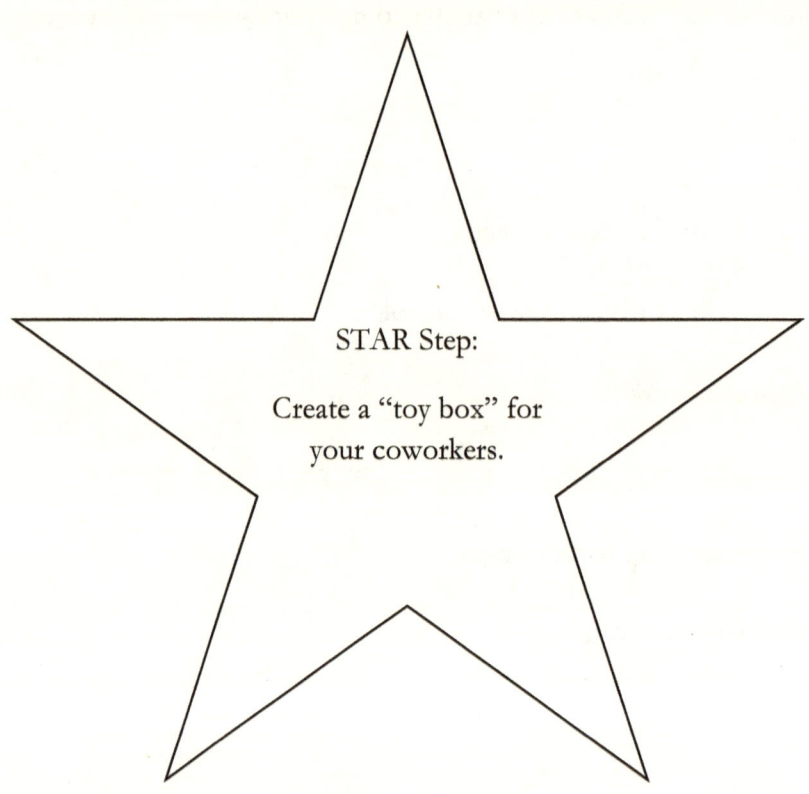

STAR Step:

Create a "toy box" for your coworkers.

CHAPTER 12 – 12 PERKS THAT GO BEYOND PAID TIME OFF OR INSURANCE BENEFITS

If you are in a position of influence, or you can make suggestions to someone who is, here are some ways a company can offer benefits beyond what is traditionally offered.

1. Granting an *Employee of the Month* parking spot

2. Stocking the break room with fancier snacks, coffees, and teas than you would normally expect

3. Giving out vouchers/coupons

4. Supplying useful items imprinted with your logo such as mugs, pens, mouse pads

5. Providing spending allowance for company clothing each year

6. Allowing employees to play music in their workspace (if agreeable to all)

7. Furnishing ergonomic chairs, wrist rests, ear plugs

8. Reimbursing costs for a monthly gym membership

9. Helping with cell phone costs if employees use their personal phone for work-related conversations

10. Giving books and professional development materials to employees

11. Sending employees to a retreat, conference, or lunch-and-learn seminar

12. Provide nice decor options for cubicles and offices, such as plants, allowance to buy a painting, etc.

All the perks in the world do not replace common courtesy, respect, and realistic expectations.

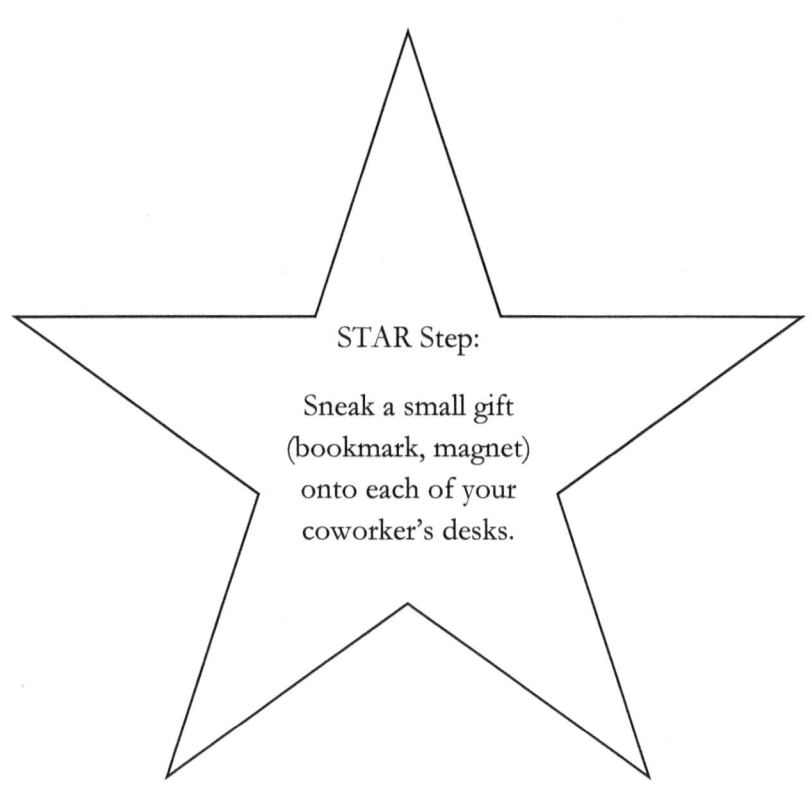

STAR Step:

Sneak a small gift (bookmark, magnet) onto each of your coworker's desks.

CHAPTER 13 – 12 RESOURCES FOR BOOSTING WORKPLACE MORALE

Here are 12 websites, books, and resources you can look to for more details and ideas about boosting workplace morale. Sites were active as of the publication of this book in 2014. Inclusion of a site does not imply that I endorse all contents of the site.

1. *BethBeutler.com* – I offer blog posts, downloadable resources, and teambuilding consultations. Downloads include:

- A Bible study on "Strife vs. Peace" for faith-based organizations to use with their staff
- A 12-Minute Personality Test (non-scientific, but great to prompt discussion.)
- Reproducible game sheets such as BINGO and scavenger hunt lists

There is a small fee for each download, which allows you a master copy and the permission to duplicate it for use within one organization or community group.

2. *CCTBusiness.com* – offering business soft skill classes that include motivation and leadership. Mention my name if you contact them.

3. *HDRQstore.com* – resources for trainers and leaders

4. *Orientaltrading.com* – extensive source of supplies, small gifts, decorations, and more

5. *Baudville.com* – gifts and awards for recognition and team morale

6. *Big Book of Teambuilding Games* by John Newstrom and Edward Scannell. This book is listed in the Amazon store at my site. Should you choose to buy it there, I'll receive a small portion of your purchase.

7. *Bowperson.com* – website of Sharon Bowman, who believes in making training fun

8. *Riverstoneway.com* – leadership development; DISC assessments (should you retain them, please mention that Beth Beutler sent you their way.)

9. *Different Children Different Needs* by Charles Boyd. Although this book is for parents, its insights into adapting your approaches to the different styles of children can be applied to just about any relationship. Charlie is also my pastor. This book is also in my Amazon store.

10. *Despair.com* – this site offers tongue-in-cheek products that parody motivational products. Can be fun for a laugh.

11. *4imprint.com* – great site for obtaining giveaways that can be imprinted with your company logo. Love this company! Their "Blue Box" sampler is also a lot of fun.

12. *Google.com* – this might be obvious, but all you have to do to find tons of ideas and information is to search with terms such as "teambuilding" and "teambuilding activities." Also, Google has a reputation for having an upbeat, generous workplace culture, so check out some of their practices.

One company that offers unique benefits (among many) is Buffer. Check out www.bufferapp.com. Their team is located all over the world yet they build cohesiveness in unique ways.

STAR Step:

Keep this book handy
and refer to it regularly.

ABOUT THE AUTHOR

Beth Beutler is an author, speaker, virtual assistant and consultant who brings hope to busy, stressed, and principle-centered people. She helps them excel in personal growth, inspired thinking, team building, productivity, communication and the enjoyment of refreshing experiences so they can generously help other people excel.

Thank you very much for obtaining my book. I hope you see that everyone in the workplace, whether a named team leader or not, can contribute to the environment and spirit of the workplace.

I'd love to hear if/how some of these ideas have influenced your culture. Contact me through *www.BethBeutler.com* where you can also receive a free e-book for joining my email list.

www.ingramcontent.com/pod-product-compliance
Lightning Source LLC
Chambersburg PA
CBHW021441170526
45164CB00001B/344